Fifth Position
for the Cello

by Cassia Harvey

cover drawing
Spring Enigmas
Greg Harvey
(pen-and-ink)

CHP198

©2009 by C. Harvey Publications® All Rights Reserved.
www.charveypublications.com - print books and free sheet music blog
www.learnstrings.com - PDF downloadable books and chamber music

Fifth Position for the Cello

Cassia Harvey

Note:
I = A String
II = D String
III = G String
IV = C String

I. D string studies with 1st and 2nd fingers

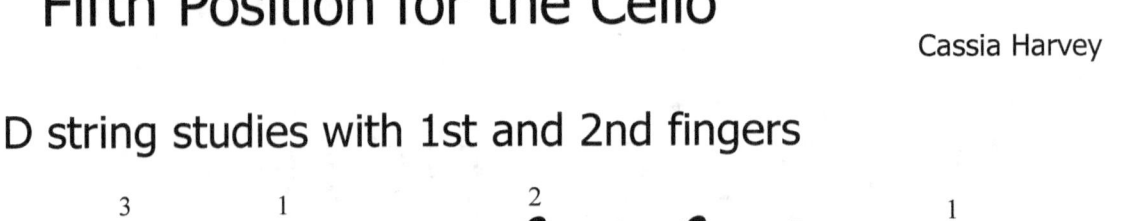

Finger Exercise

©2008 C. Harvey Publications All Rights Reserved.

Shifting

Old Tune

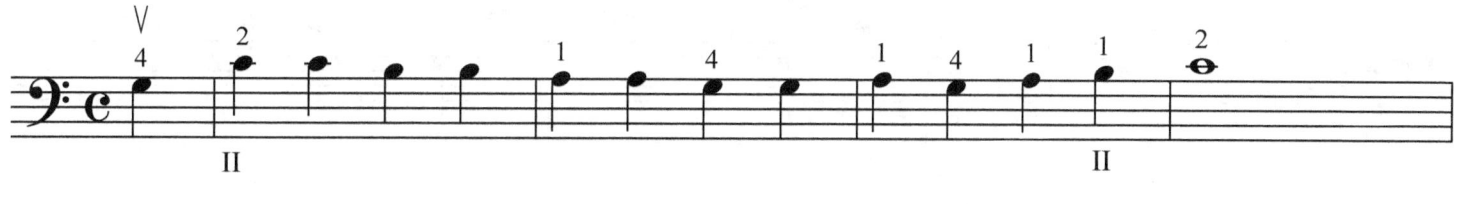

Portuguese Folk Song

©2008 C. Harvey Publications All Rights Reserved.

Frere Jacques Variations

III. Third finger on the D and A strings

Shifting Exercise

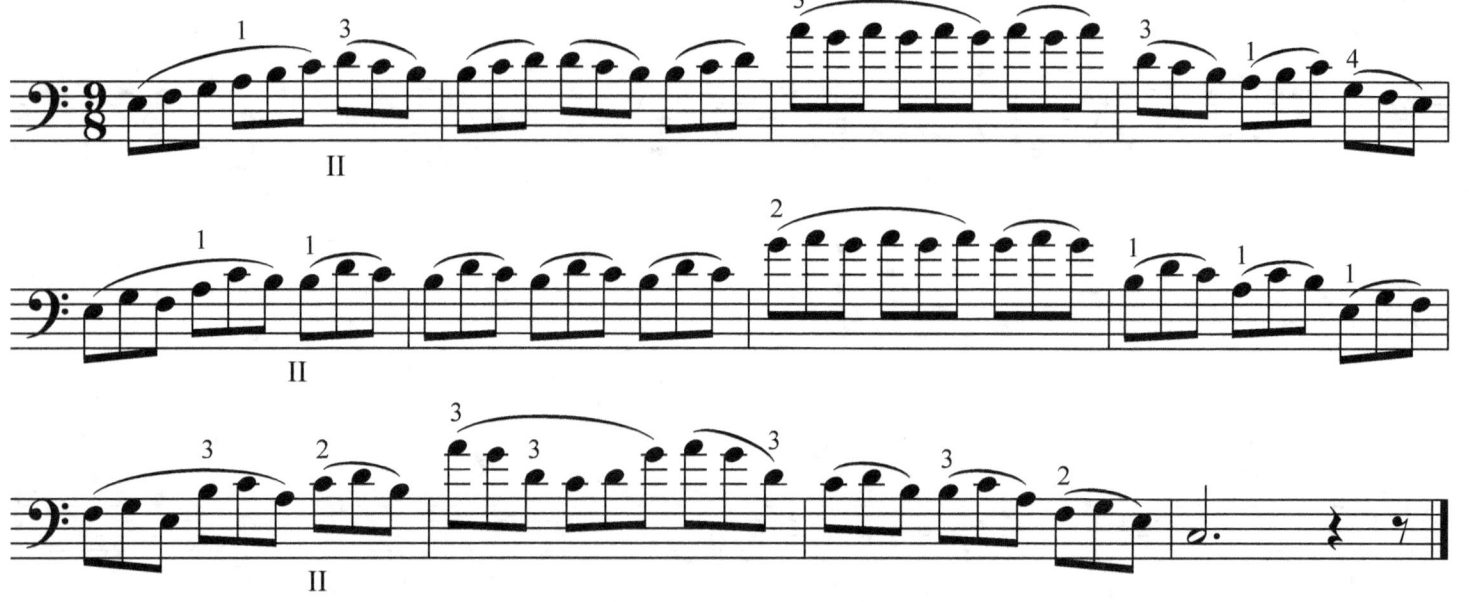

IV. The A string notes in fifth position

V. Crossing strings in fifth position

Fifth Position for the Cello

English Dance
Traditional, arr. Harvey

Ballet Music
Bast, arr. Harvey

©2008 C. Harvey Publications All Rights Reserved.

VI. Shifting to fifth position

Fifth Position for the Cello

Folk Song

Jig

Bast, arr. Harvey

©2008 C. Harvey Publications All Rights Reserved.

VII. The notes on the G string

Fifth Position for the Cello

Minuet and Rondeau
Rameau, arr. Harvey

Russian Folk Song
Traditional, arr. Harvey

©2008 C. Harvey Publications All Rights Reserved.

VIII. Low first finger; reaching 2 whole steps

18

IX. Across the strings with 2 whole steps

Fifth Position for the Cello

The C string

Fifth Position for the Cello

Allegro

Albrecht, arr. Harvey

Allegro from Horn Concerto

Mozart, arr. Harvey

©2008 C. Harvey Publications All Rights Reserved.

Funeral of the Bird

Cuis, arr. Harvey

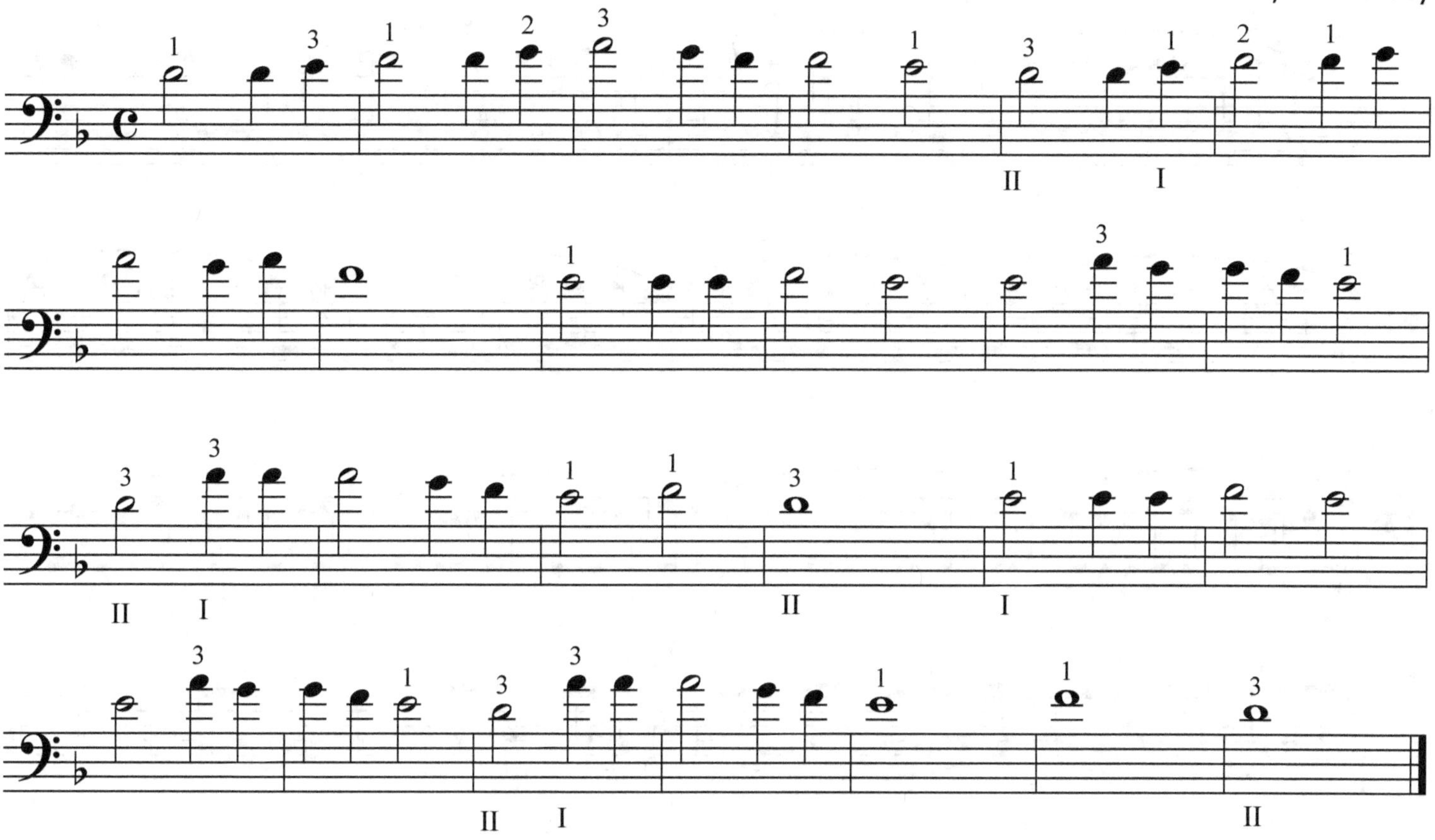

La Chasse

Biehl, arr. Harvey

XI. Switching between Stretched and Closed Positions

Changing Finger Positions Across Strings

Fifth Position for the Cello

English Dance

Bast, arr. Harvey

Allegretto

Donizetti, arr. Harvey

©2008 C. Harvey Publications All Rights Reserved.

XII. High 2nd Finger

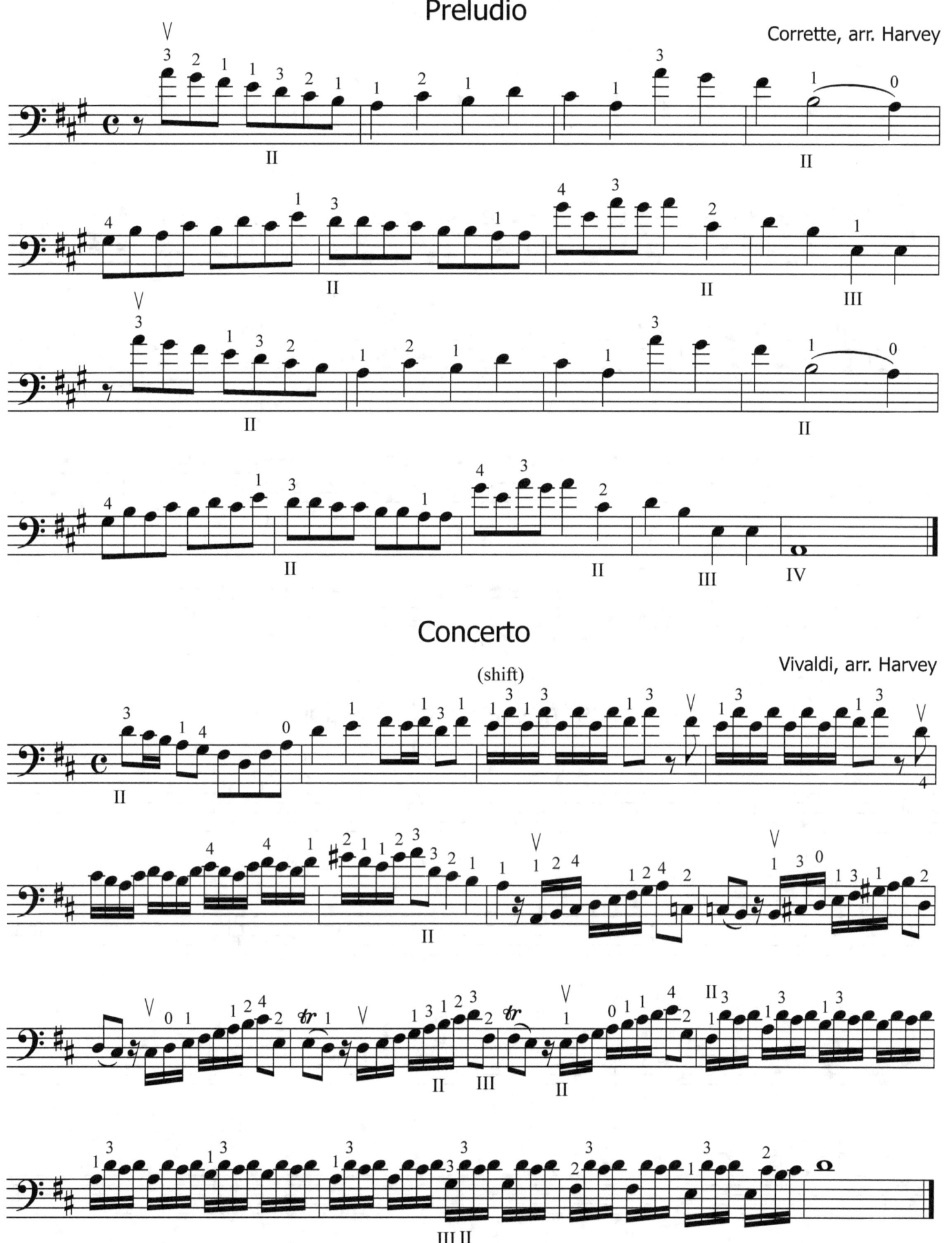

XIII. Across strings

Scales that use Fifth Position

Fifth Position for the Cello

Russian Folk Song

Traditional, arr. Harvey

La Tarantelle

Burgmuller, arr. Harvey

©2008 C. Harvey Publications All Rights Reserved.

XIV. Low 1st Finger and High 2nd Finger

Trill Exercise

D string

©2008 C. Harvey Publications All Rights Reserved.

Fifth Position for the Cello

29

La Supplication

Biehl, arr. Harvey

Arietta

Carissimi, arr. Harvey

©2008 C. Harvey Publications All Rights Reserved.

Different Finger Positions

Fifth Position for the Cello

©2008 C. Harvey Publications All Rights Reserved.

Fifth Position for the Cello

Etude

Wohlfahrt, arr. Harvey

©2008 C. Harvey Publications All Rights Reserved.

Double Stops

Fifth Position for the Cello

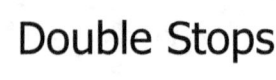

Fifth Position for the Cello

Study

Beyer, arr. Harvey

Folk Tune

Traditional, arr. Harvey

©2008 C. Harvey Publications All Rights Reserved.

Other Finger Patterns

Fifth Position for the Cello

Oh Susannah

Foster, arr. Harvey

Lesson

Azais, arr. Harvey

©2008 C. Harvey Publications All Rights Reserved.

Finger Patterns with Fourth Finger

Fifth Position for the Cello

Fifth Position for the Cello

Study

Beyer, arr. Harvey

Romanze

Jensen, arr. Harvey

©2008 C. Harvey Publications All Rights Reserved.

Fifth Position with Seventh Position

Fifth Position for the Cello

Grandfather's Waltz

Behr, arr. Harvey

Sonata

Marcello, arr. Harvey

©2008 C. Harvey Publications All Rights Reserved.

Fifth Position for the Cello
41

Allegretto
Beyer, arr. Harvey

Allegro
Vogt, arr. Harvey

©2008 C. Harvey Publications All Rights Reserved.

C Major Patterns

Allegro
Marcello, arr. Harvey

©2008 C. Harvey Publications All Rights Reserved.

Fifth Position for the Cello

G Major Patterns

Vivace

Raoul, arr. Harvey

©2008 C. Harvey Publications All Rights Reserved.

D Major Patterns

Miss Ratray's Reel

Traditional, arr. Harvey

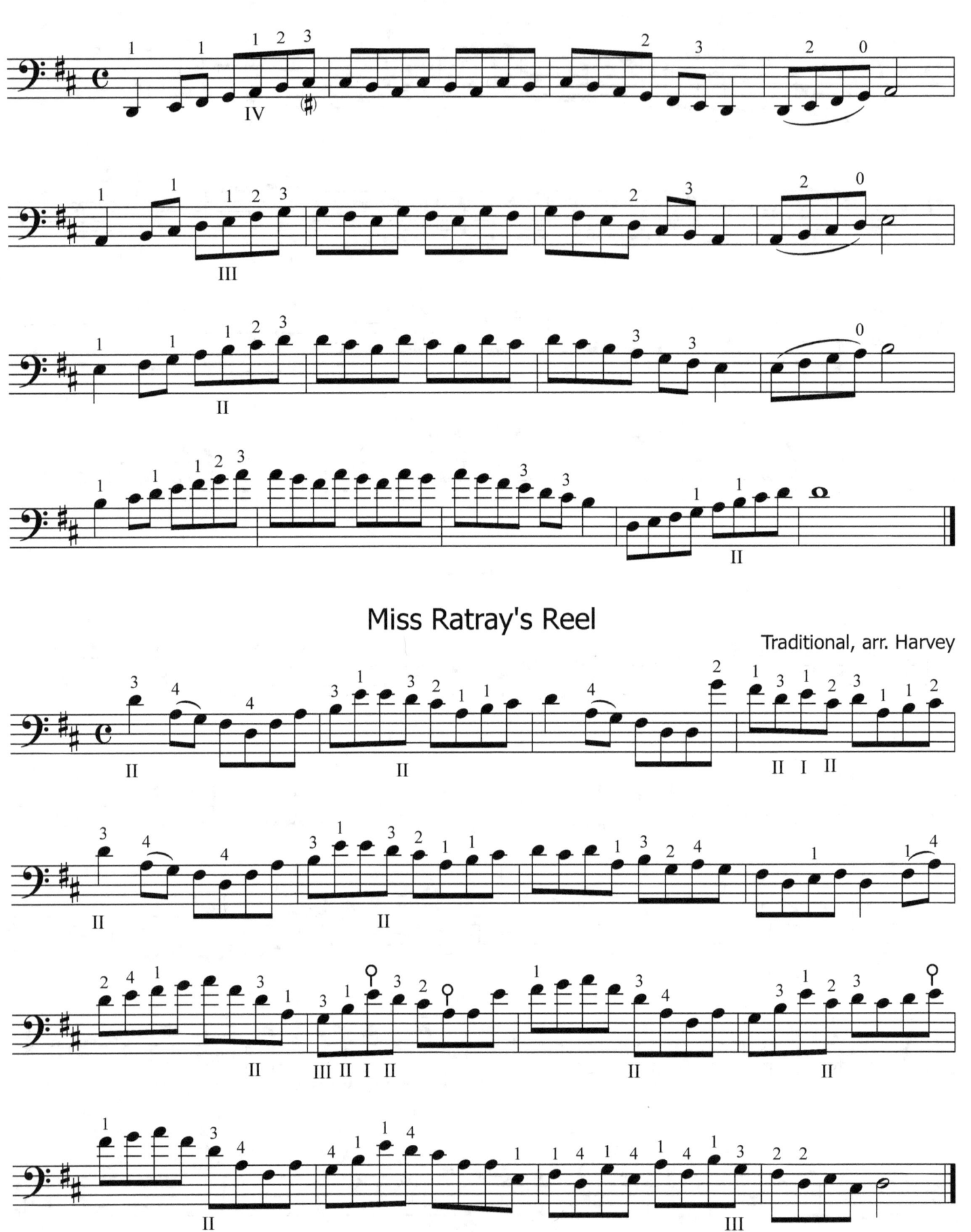

Fifth Position for the Cello
45

F Major Patterns

Concerto Theme

Telemann, arr. Harvey

©2008 C. Harvey Publications All Rights Reserved.

G Scales

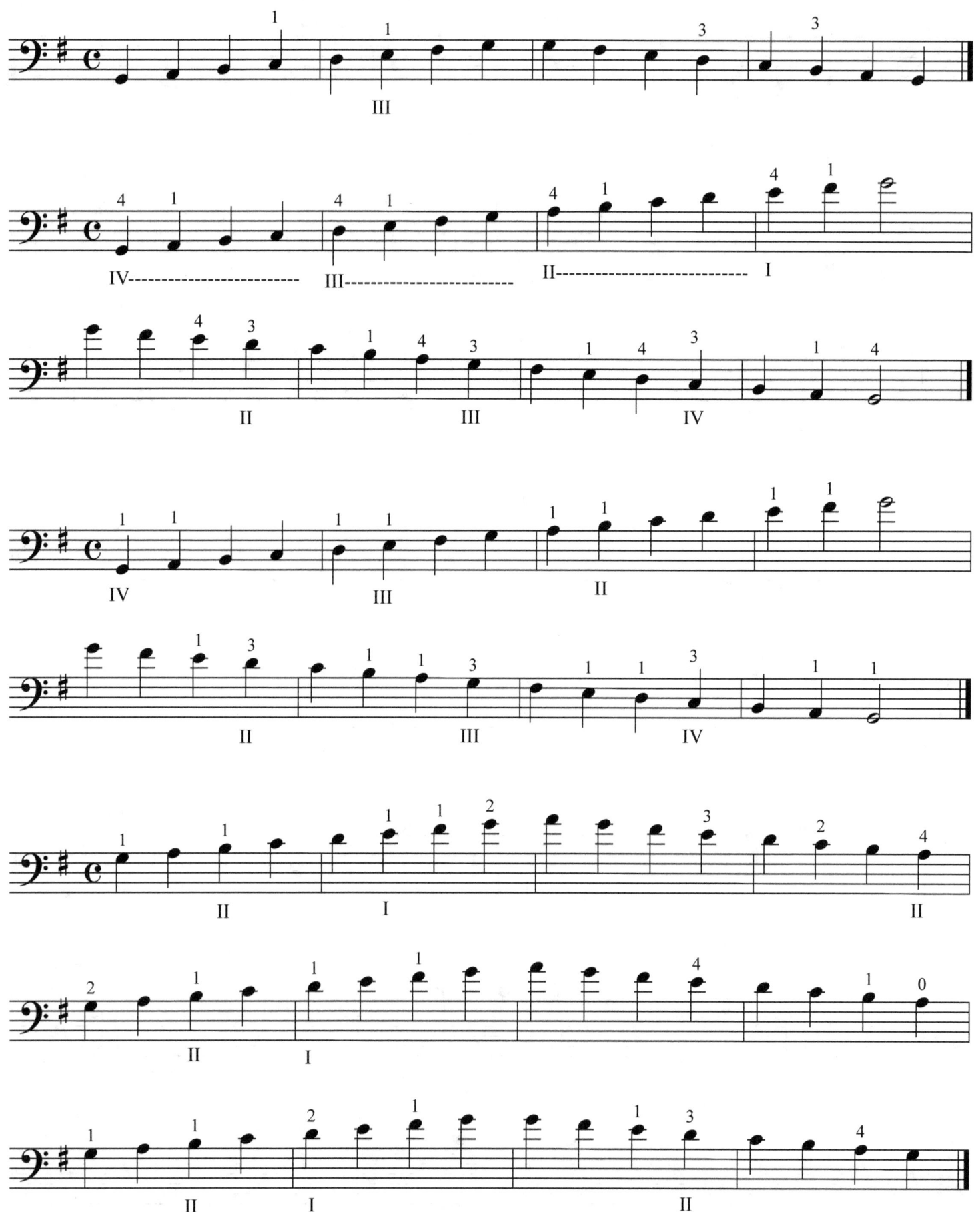

Fifth Position for the Cello

D Scales

©2008 C. Harvey Publications All Rights Reserved.

50

F Scales

Fifth Position for the Cello

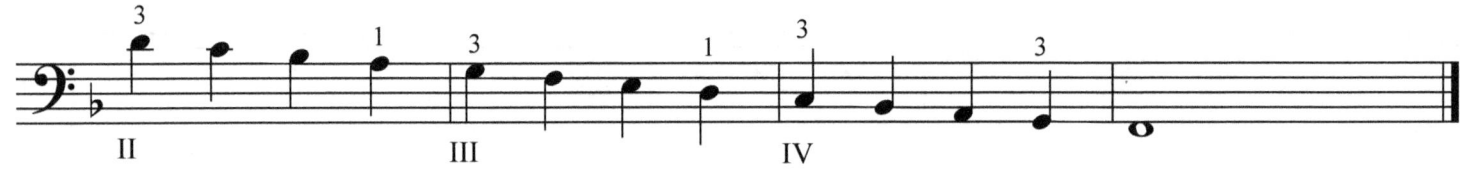

©2008 C. Harvey Publications All Rights Reserved.

Fifth Position for the Cello

B♭ Scales

©2008 C. Harvey Publications All Rights Reserved.

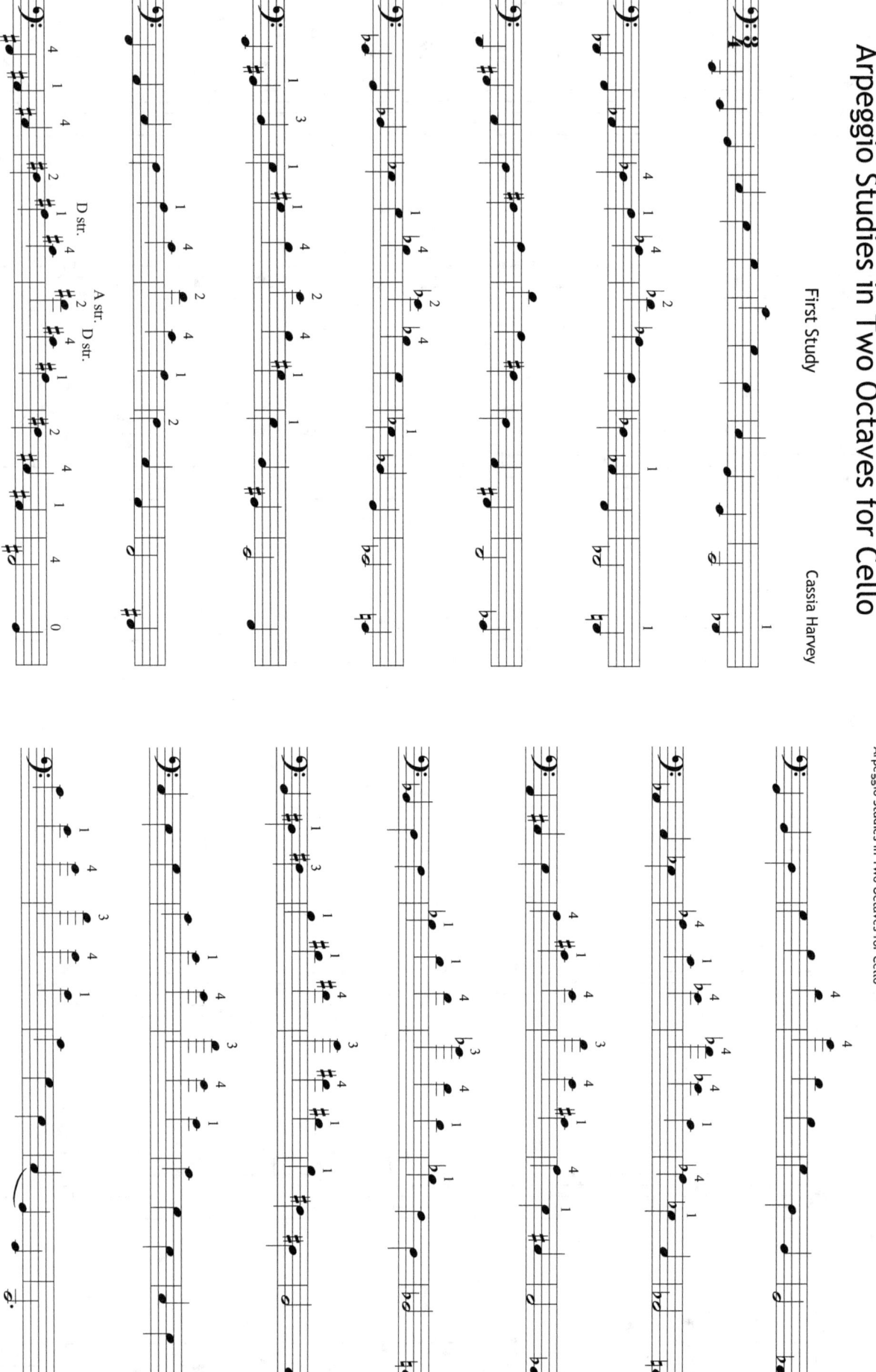

available from **www.charveypublications.com**: CHP319
The Fauré Élégie Study Book for Cello